50 Grilled Meat Barbecue Dishes

By: Kelly Johnson

Table of Contents

- BBQ Ribs
- Grilled Chicken Wings
- Pulled Pork
- Beef Brisket
- Grilled Steak
- Grilled Sausages
- BBQ Chicken
- Grilled Lamb Chops
- Grilled Pork Chops
- Grilled Shrimp Skewers
- Grilled Beef Kebabs
- BBQ Meatballs
- Grilled Pork Tenderloin
- Grilled Turkey Burgers
- Grilled Hot Dogs
- Grilled T-bone Steak
- BBQ Short Ribs
- Grilled Skirt Steak
- Grilled Veal Chops

- Grilled Salmon
- Grilled Veggie and Meat Skewers
- Grilled Chicken Thighs
- BBQ Beef Ribs
- Grilled Duck Breast
- BBQ Pulled Chicken
- Grilled Lamb Shanks
- BBQ Bacon-wrapped Shrimp
- Grilled Fish Tacos
- Grilled Bratwurst
- Grilled Porterhouse Steak
- BBQ Hot Link Sausages
- Grilled Spicy Chicken Drumsticks
- Grilled Beef Tri-Tip
- BBQ Venison Ribs
- Grilled Marinated Pork Belly
- Grilled Lamb Kofta
- Grilled Flank Steak
- BBQ Baby Back Ribs
- Grilled Duck Legs
- BBQ Mutton Chops

- Grilled Chicken Kebabs
- Grilled Tri-Tip Roast
- BBQ Shredded Beef
- Grilled Teriyaki Chicken
- Grilled Ribeye Steak
- BBQ Pork Burnt Ends
- Grilled Italian Sausages
- Grilled Beef Filet Mignon
- BBQ Chicken Sandwiches
- Grilled Cornish Hens

BBQ Ribs

Ingredients:

- 2 racks of baby back ribs
- 1/4 cup brown sugar
- 2 tbsp paprika
- 1 tbsp black pepper
- 1 tbsp salt
- 1 tsp garlic powder
- 1 tsp onion powder
- 1 tsp cayenne pepper
- 1/2 cup BBQ sauce

Instructions:

1. Preheat the grill to medium heat.
2. Remove the membrane from the ribs and pat them dry with paper towels.
3. In a small bowl, mix brown sugar, paprika, black pepper, salt, garlic powder, onion powder, and cayenne pepper.
4. Rub the seasoning mixture evenly over both sides of the ribs.
5. Place the ribs on the grill, bone-side down, and cook for 2-3 hours, occasionally flipping and basting with BBQ sauce.
6. During the last 15 minutes of cooking, coat the ribs with BBQ sauce.
7. Remove from the grill, let rest for 10 minutes, and serve.

Grilled Chicken Wings

Ingredients:

- 12 chicken wings
- 2 tbsp olive oil
- 1 tsp garlic powder
- 1 tsp onion powder
- 1 tsp smoked paprika
- 1/2 tsp salt
- 1/2 tsp black pepper
- 1/4 cup BBQ sauce (optional)

Instructions:

1. Preheat the grill to medium-high heat.
2. In a bowl, toss the chicken wings with olive oil, garlic powder, onion powder, paprika, salt, and black pepper.
3. Grill the wings for 20-25 minutes, flipping occasionally until golden brown and cooked through.
4. If desired, during the last few minutes of grilling, brush with BBQ sauce.
5. Remove from the grill, let rest, and serve.

Pulled Pork

Ingredients:

- 4 lb pork shoulder (bone-in or boneless)
- 1/4 cup brown sugar
- 1 tbsp paprika
- 1 tbsp salt
- 1 tbsp black pepper
- 1 tsp garlic powder
- 1 tsp onion powder
- 1 tsp cumin
- 1/2 tsp cayenne pepper
- 1 cup apple cider vinegar
- 1 cup BBQ sauce

Instructions:

1. Preheat the grill or smoker to 225°F (107°C).
2. In a bowl, combine brown sugar, paprika, salt, pepper, garlic powder, onion powder, cumin, and cayenne pepper.
3. Rub the seasoning mixture over the pork shoulder.
4. Place the pork on the grill or smoker, fat-side up, and cook for 6-8 hours, or until the internal temperature reaches 195°F (90°C).
5. Once cooked, remove the pork and rest for 10-15 minutes.
6. Shred the pork using two forks and toss with apple cider vinegar and BBQ sauce.

7. Serve with your favorite sides or on buns.

Beef Brisket

Ingredients:

- 5 lb beef brisket
- 1/4 cup brown sugar
- 1/4 cup paprika
- 1 tbsp black pepper
- 1 tbsp salt
- 1 tbsp garlic powder
- 1 tbsp onion powder
- 1 tsp cumin
- 1/2 tsp cayenne pepper
- 1 cup beef broth

Instructions:

1. Preheat the smoker or grill to 225°F (107°C).
2. In a bowl, mix brown sugar, paprika, black pepper, salt, garlic powder, onion powder, cumin, and cayenne pepper.
3. Rub the seasoning mixture evenly over the brisket.
4. Place the brisket on the grill or smoker, fat-side up, and cook for 10-12 hours, or until the internal temperature reaches 195°F (90°C).
5. Periodically spritz with beef broth to keep moist.
6. Once cooked, remove the brisket and let rest for 30 minutes.
7. Slice thinly and serve.

Grilled Steak

Ingredients:

- 2 rib-eye steaks (or your favorite cut)
- 2 tbsp olive oil
- 1 tsp garlic powder
- 1 tsp rosemary (optional)
- Salt and pepper to taste

Instructions:

1. Preheat the grill to high heat.
2. Rub the steaks with olive oil, garlic powder, rosemary, salt, and pepper.
3. Grill the steaks for 4-5 minutes per side for medium-rare, or longer for desired doneness.
4. Remove the steaks from the grill and let rest for 5 minutes before serving.

Grilled Sausages

Ingredients:

- 4 sausages (your choice of type)
- 1 tbsp olive oil
- 1/2 tsp garlic powder
- 1/2 tsp onion powder
- 1/2 tsp paprika
- Salt and pepper to taste

Instructions:

1. Preheat the grill to medium heat.
2. Rub the sausages with olive oil and season with garlic powder, onion powder, paprika, salt, and pepper.
3. Grill the sausages for 10-12 minutes, turning occasionally until browned and cooked through.
4. Serve with grilled vegetables or in a bun.

BBQ Chicken

Ingredients:

- 4 chicken breasts or thighs
- 1/4 cup BBQ sauce
- Salt and pepper to taste

Instructions:

1. Preheat the grill to medium heat.
2. Season the chicken with salt and pepper.
3. Grill the chicken for 6-7 minutes per side, basting with BBQ sauce during the last few minutes of cooking.
4. Check for doneness with a meat thermometer (165°F/74°C).
5. Let rest for 5 minutes before serving.

Grilled Lamb Chops

Ingredients:

- 8 lamb chops
- 2 tbsp olive oil
- 2 garlic cloves, minced
- 1 tsp rosemary
- Salt and pepper to taste

Instructions:

1. Preheat the grill to medium-high heat.
2. In a bowl, mix olive oil, garlic, rosemary, salt, and pepper.
3. Coat the lamb chops with the marinade and let sit for 15-20 minutes.
4. Grill the lamb chops for 4-5 minutes per side for medium-rare, or longer for desired doneness.
5. Let rest for 5 minutes before serving.

Grilled Pork Chops

Ingredients:

- 4 bone-in pork chops
- 1 tbsp olive oil
- 1 tsp garlic powder
- 1 tsp paprika
- 1/2 tsp salt
- 1/2 tsp black pepper

Instructions:

1. Preheat the grill to medium-high heat.
2. Rub the pork chops with olive oil and season with garlic powder, paprika, salt, and black pepper.
3. Grill the pork chops for 5-7 minutes per side, or until the internal temperature reaches 145°F (63°C).
4. Let rest for 5 minutes before serving.

Grilled Shrimp Skewers

Ingredients:

- 1 lb large shrimp, peeled and deveined
- 2 tbsp olive oil
- 2 garlic cloves, minced
- 1 tbsp lemon juice
- 1 tsp smoked paprika
- Salt and pepper to taste
- Fresh parsley for garnish

Instructions:

1. Preheat the grill to medium-high heat.
2. In a bowl, toss the shrimp with olive oil, garlic, lemon juice, paprika, salt, and pepper.
3. Thread the shrimp onto skewers.
4. Grill the shrimp for 2-3 minutes per side, or until opaque and slightly charred.
5. Garnish with fresh parsley and serve.

Grilled Beef Kebabs

Ingredients:

- 1 lb beef sirloin or tenderloin, cut into cubes
- 1 red bell pepper, cut into chunks
- 1 onion, cut into chunks
- 1 zucchini, cut into chunks
- 2 tbsp olive oil
- 1 tsp garlic powder
- 1 tsp dried oregano
- Salt and pepper to taste

Instructions:

1. Preheat the grill to medium-high heat.
2. In a bowl, combine the beef cubes, bell pepper, onion, and zucchini.
3. Drizzle with olive oil, then sprinkle with garlic powder, oregano, salt, and pepper. Toss to coat.
4. Thread the beef and vegetables onto skewers.
5. Grill for 8-10 minutes, turning occasionally, until the beef is cooked to your desired doneness.
6. Serve immediately.

BBQ Meatballs

Ingredients:

- 1 lb ground beef or pork
- 1/2 cup breadcrumbs
- 1/4 cup grated Parmesan cheese
- 1 egg
- 2 garlic cloves, minced
- 1/4 cup parsley, chopped
- 1 cup BBQ sauce

Instructions:

1. Preheat the grill to medium heat.
2. In a bowl, combine the ground meat, breadcrumbs, Parmesan, egg, garlic, and parsley.
3. Form the mixture into meatballs.
4. Place the meatballs on the grill, turning frequently, for 10-12 minutes until fully cooked.
5. During the last few minutes, brush the meatballs with BBQ sauce and cook for an additional 2 minutes.
6. Serve hot with extra BBQ sauce.

Grilled Pork Tenderloin

Ingredients:

- 1 lb pork tenderloin
- 2 tbsp olive oil
- 1 tsp garlic powder
- 1 tsp onion powder
- 1 tsp smoked paprika
- Salt and pepper to taste

Instructions:

1. Preheat the grill to medium-high heat.
2. Rub the pork tenderloin with olive oil and season with garlic powder, onion powder, paprika, salt, and pepper.
3. Grill the pork for 20-25 minutes, turning occasionally, until the internal temperature reaches 145°F (63°C).
4. Let the pork rest for 5-10 minutes before slicing and serving.

Grilled Turkey Burgers

Ingredients:

- 1 lb ground turkey
- 1/4 cup breadcrumbs
- 1/4 cup grated Parmesan cheese
- 1 egg
- 1 tsp garlic powder
- 1/2 tsp salt
- 1/4 tsp black pepper

Instructions:

1. Preheat the grill to medium heat.
2. In a bowl, combine ground turkey, breadcrumbs, Parmesan, egg, garlic powder, salt, and pepper.
3. Shape the mixture into 4 patties.
4. Grill the patties for 5-7 minutes per side until the internal temperature reaches 165°F (74°C).
5. Serve on buns with your favorite toppings.

Grilled Hot Dogs

Ingredients:

- 4 hot dogs
- 4 hot dog buns
- Condiments of choice (mustard, ketchup, relish, etc.)

Instructions:

1. Preheat the grill to medium heat.
2. Grill the hot dogs for 5-7 minutes, turning occasionally, until heated through and slightly charred.
3. Place the hot dogs in buns and add your favorite condiments.
4. Serve immediately.

Grilled T-bone Steak

Ingredients:

- 2 T-bone steaks
- 2 tbsp olive oil
- 1 tsp garlic powder
- 1 tsp rosemary
- Salt and pepper to taste

Instructions:

1. Preheat the grill to high heat.
2. Rub the steaks with olive oil and season with garlic powder, rosemary, salt, and pepper.
3. Grill the steaks for 4-5 minutes per side for medium-rare, or longer for your desired doneness.
4. Remove from the grill and let rest for 5 minutes before serving.

BBQ Short Ribs

Ingredients:

- 4 lbs beef short ribs
- 1/4 cup brown sugar
- 2 tbsp paprika
- 1 tbsp garlic powder
- 1 tbsp onion powder
- 1 tsp cayenne pepper
- 1 cup BBQ sauce

Instructions:

1. Preheat the grill to medium heat.
2. In a bowl, mix brown sugar, paprika, garlic powder, onion powder, and cayenne pepper.
3. Rub the seasoning mix over the short ribs.
4. Grill the ribs for 3-4 hours, turning occasionally and basting with BBQ sauce during the last hour.
5. Remove from the grill, let rest, and serve.

Grilled Skirt Steak

Ingredients:

- 1 lb skirt steak
- 2 tbsp olive oil
- 2 tbsp soy sauce
- 1 tbsp garlic, minced
- 1 tbsp lime juice
- 1 tsp cumin
- Salt and pepper to taste

Instructions:

1. Preheat the grill to medium-high heat.
2. In a bowl, whisk together olive oil, soy sauce, garlic, lime juice, cumin, salt, and pepper.
3. Marinate the skirt steak for 30 minutes to 1 hour.
4. Grill the steak for 3-4 minutes per side for medium-rare, or longer for your desired doneness.
5. Let the steak rest for 5 minutes before slicing against the grain and serving.

Grilled Veal Chops

Ingredients:

- 4 veal chops
- 2 tbsp olive oil
- 2 garlic cloves, minced
- 1 tsp rosemary
- Salt and pepper to taste

Instructions:

1. Preheat the grill to medium-high heat.
2. Rub the veal chops with olive oil, garlic, rosemary, salt, and pepper.
3. Grill the veal chops for 5-7 minutes per side for medium, or longer for your desired doneness.
4. Let the chops rest for 5 minutes before serving.

Grilled Salmon

Ingredients:

- 4 salmon fillets
- 2 tbsp olive oil
- 1 lemon, thinly sliced
- 1 tbsp fresh dill, chopped
- Salt and pepper to taste

Instructions:

1. Preheat the grill to medium-high heat.
2. Brush the salmon fillets with olive oil and season with salt, pepper, and fresh dill.
3. Place lemon slices on top of the salmon.
4. Grill the salmon for 4-5 minutes per side, until it reaches an internal temperature of 145°F (63°C) and easily flakes with a fork.
5. Serve with additional lemon slices.

Grilled Veggie and Meat Skewers

Ingredients:

- 1 lb beef or chicken, cut into cubes
- 1 zucchini, sliced
- 1 red bell pepper, cut into chunks
- 1 onion, cut into chunks
- 8-10 cherry tomatoes
- 2 tbsp olive oil
- 1 tsp garlic powder
- 1 tsp paprika
- Salt and pepper to taste

Instructions:

1. Preheat the grill to medium heat.
2. Thread the meat and vegetables onto skewers.
3. Drizzle with olive oil and sprinkle with garlic powder, paprika, salt, and pepper.
4. Grill for 8-10 minutes, turning occasionally, until the meat is cooked through and the veggies are tender.
5. Serve hot with a side of rice or salad.

Grilled Chicken Thighs

Ingredients:

- 4 bone-in, skin-on chicken thighs
- 2 tbsp olive oil
- 1 tsp paprika
- 1 tsp garlic powder
- 1/2 tsp dried thyme
- Salt and pepper to taste

Instructions:

1. Preheat the grill to medium heat.
2. Rub the chicken thighs with olive oil and season with paprika, garlic powder, thyme, salt, and pepper.
3. Grill the chicken for 7-8 minutes per side, or until the internal temperature reaches 165°F (74°C).
4. Let the chicken rest for a few minutes before serving.

BBQ Beef Ribs

Ingredients:

- 2 racks of beef ribs
- 1/4 cup brown sugar
- 1 tbsp paprika
- 1 tbsp garlic powder
- 1 tbsp onion powder
- 1 tsp chili powder
- Salt and pepper to taste
- 2 cups BBQ sauce

Instructions:

1. Preheat the grill to low heat (about 275°F or 135°C).
2. Mix the brown sugar, paprika, garlic powder, onion powder, chili powder, salt, and pepper in a bowl.
3. Rub the spice mixture all over the beef ribs.
4. Wrap the ribs in foil and grill for 2.5-3 hours, turning occasionally.
5. Unwrap the ribs and baste with BBQ sauce. Grill for an additional 10-15 minutes, flipping the ribs and basting again halfway through.
6. Let rest for 5-10 minutes before slicing and serving.

Grilled Duck Breast

Ingredients:

- 2 duck breasts
- 1 tbsp olive oil
- 1 tsp fresh thyme, chopped
- Salt and pepper to taste
- 1 tbsp honey (optional for glaze)

Instructions:

1. Preheat the grill to medium-high heat.
2. Score the skin of the duck breasts in a criss-cross pattern.
3. Rub the duck breasts with olive oil, thyme, salt, and pepper.
4. Grill the duck breasts for 5-7 minutes per side, until the skin is crispy and the internal temperature reaches 135°F (57°C) for medium-rare.
5. Optionally, drizzle with honey during the last few minutes of grilling for a sweet glaze.
6. Let the duck rest for 5 minutes before serving.

BBQ Pulled Chicken

Ingredients:

- 4 chicken breasts (boneless, skinless)
- 1 cup BBQ sauce
- 1/2 cup chicken broth
- 1 tbsp apple cider vinegar
- Salt and pepper to taste

Instructions:

1. Preheat the grill to medium heat.
2. Season the chicken breasts with salt and pepper.
3. Grill the chicken for 6-8 minutes per side, until fully cooked (internal temperature of 165°F or 74°C).
4. While the chicken is grilling, mix the BBQ sauce, chicken broth, and apple cider vinegar in a small bowl.
5. Once the chicken is cooked, shred it using two forks and mix with the BBQ sauce mixture.
6. Serve on buns with pickles or as a main dish.

Grilled Lamb Shanks

Ingredients:

- 4 lamb shanks
- 2 tbsp olive oil
- 1 tbsp garlic, minced
- 1 tbsp rosemary, chopped
- Salt and pepper to taste
- 1/2 cup red wine (optional for basting)

Instructions:

1. Preheat the grill to medium heat.
2. Rub the lamb shanks with olive oil, garlic, rosemary, salt, and pepper.
3. Grill the lamb shanks for 4-5 minutes per side, then lower the heat to medium-low.
4. Continue grilling for 45-60 minutes, turning occasionally and basting with red wine, until tender and cooked through.
5. Let the lamb rest for 5-10 minutes before serving.

BBQ Bacon-wrapped Shrimp

Ingredients:

- 1 lb large shrimp, peeled and deveined
- 8 slices of bacon
- 1/4 cup BBQ sauce
- 1 tbsp olive oil
- Salt and pepper to taste

Instructions:

1. Preheat the grill to medium-high heat.
2. Wrap each shrimp with a slice of bacon and secure with toothpicks.
3. Brush the shrimp with olive oil, salt, and pepper.
4. Grill for 2-3 minutes per side, until the bacon is crispy and the shrimp is cooked through.
5. During the last few minutes, brush with BBQ sauce for added flavor.
6. Serve hot.

Grilled Fish Tacos

Ingredients:

- 1 lb white fish fillets (tilapia, mahi-mahi, etc.)
- 1 tbsp olive oil
- 1 tsp cumin
- 1/2 tsp chili powder
- 1 lime, juiced
- Salt and pepper to taste
- 8 small corn tortillas
- Fresh cilantro, chopped
- Red cabbage, shredded
- Sour cream (optional)

Instructions:

1. Preheat the grill to medium-high heat.
2. Rub the fish fillets with olive oil, cumin, chili powder, lime juice, salt, and pepper.
3. Grill the fish for 3-4 minutes per side until cooked through and easily flaked.
4. Warm the tortillas on the grill for about 30 seconds.
5. Flake the grilled fish and place on the tortillas.
6. Top with shredded cabbage, fresh cilantro, and a dollop of sour cream.
7. Serve immediately.

Grilled Bratwurst

Ingredients:

- 4 bratwurst sausages
- 1 onion, sliced
- 1 tbsp olive oil
- 1 tbsp mustard
- 1 tsp paprika
- Salt and pepper to taste
- 4 buns, for serving

Instructions:

1. Preheat the grill to medium heat.
2. Lightly oil the grill grates to prevent sticking.
3. Grill the bratwurst sausages for about 6-8 minutes per side until browned and cooked through.
4. In the last few minutes of grilling, brush the sausages with mustard and sprinkle with paprika for extra flavor.
5. Grill the onion slices until tender and caramelized.
6. Serve the bratwurst in buns with grilled onions and your favorite condiments.

Grilled Porterhouse Steak

Ingredients:

- 2 porterhouse steaks
- 2 tbsp olive oil
- 2 cloves garlic, minced
- 1 tbsp fresh rosemary, chopped
- Salt and pepper to taste
- 1 tbsp butter (optional)

Instructions:

1. Preheat the grill to high heat.
2. Rub the steaks with olive oil, garlic, rosemary, salt, and pepper.
3. Grill the steaks for 4-6 minutes per side for medium-rare, or until your desired doneness is reached.
4. Optional: In the last minute of grilling, add a small piece of butter on top of each steak for extra richness.
5. Let the steaks rest for 5 minutes before serving.

BBQ Hot Link Sausages

Ingredients:

- 4 hot link sausages
- 1/2 cup BBQ sauce
- 1 tsp cayenne pepper (optional for extra heat)
- 1 tbsp honey (optional for sweetness)

Instructions:

1. Preheat the grill to medium-high heat.
2. Grill the hot link sausages for 6-8 minutes, turning occasionally, until browned and cooked through.
3. In the last 2 minutes of grilling, brush the sausages with BBQ sauce mixed with cayenne pepper and honey for a smoky, spicy kick.
4. Serve with additional BBQ sauce on the side.

Grilled Spicy Chicken Drumsticks

Ingredients:

- 8 chicken drumsticks
- 2 tbsp olive oil
- 1 tbsp chili powder
- 1 tsp cayenne pepper
- 1 tsp garlic powder
- 1 tsp smoked paprika
- Salt and pepper to taste

Instructions:

1. Preheat the grill to medium heat.
2. Rub the drumsticks with olive oil, chili powder, cayenne pepper, garlic powder, smoked paprika, salt, and pepper.
3. Grill the drumsticks for 10-12 minutes per side, turning occasionally, until cooked through and the internal temperature reaches 165°F (74°C).
4. Serve with a side of ranch dressing or a cooling dipping sauce.

Grilled Beef Tri-Tip

Ingredients:

- 1 tri-tip roast (about 2 pounds)
- 2 tbsp olive oil
- 1 tbsp garlic powder
- 1 tbsp onion powder
- 1 tbsp smoked paprika
- 1 tsp ground cumin
- Salt and pepper to taste

Instructions:

1. Preheat the grill to medium-high heat.
2. Rub the tri-tip roast with olive oil, garlic powder, onion powder, smoked paprika, cumin, salt, and pepper.
3. Grill the roast for 25-30 minutes, turning occasionally, until the internal temperature reaches 130-135°F (54-57°C) for medium-rare.
4. Let the tri-tip rest for 10 minutes before slicing against the grain.
5. Serve with your favorite sides, like grilled vegetables or mashed potatoes.

BBQ Venison Ribs

Ingredients:

- 2 racks of venison ribs
- 1/4 cup olive oil
- 1/4 cup soy sauce
- 2 tbsp brown sugar
- 1 tbsp garlic powder
- 1 tbsp onion powder
- 1 tsp smoked paprika
- Salt and pepper to taste
- 1 cup BBQ sauce

Instructions:

1. Preheat the grill to medium-low heat.
2. Mix the olive oil, soy sauce, brown sugar, garlic powder, onion powder, smoked paprika, salt, and pepper in a bowl.
3. Rub the venison ribs with the marinade and let sit for 30 minutes.
4. Grill the ribs for 2-3 hours, turning occasionally, until tender and cooked through.
5. In the last 10 minutes of grilling, baste the ribs with BBQ sauce for added flavor.
6. Let the ribs rest for 5 minutes before slicing and serving.

Grilled Marinated Pork Belly

Ingredients:

- 1 lb pork belly, cut into strips
- 2 tbsp soy sauce
- 2 tbsp honey
- 1 tbsp rice vinegar
- 2 cloves garlic, minced
- 1 tbsp fresh ginger, grated
- 1/2 tsp chili flakes (optional)
- Salt and pepper to taste

Instructions:

1. Preheat the grill to medium heat.
2. Mix the soy sauce, honey, rice vinegar, garlic, ginger, chili flakes, salt, and pepper in a bowl.
3. Marinate the pork belly strips in the sauce for at least 30 minutes.
4. Grill the pork belly strips for 3-4 minutes per side, until crispy and cooked through.
5. Serve with a side of steamed rice or grilled vegetables.

Grilled Lamb Kofta

Ingredients:

- 1 lb ground lamb
- 1/4 cup onion, finely chopped
- 2 cloves garlic, minced
- 1 tbsp ground cumin
- 1 tsp ground coriander
- 1 tsp ground cinnamon
- 1/2 tsp ground paprika
- Salt and pepper to taste
- Fresh parsley, chopped (for garnish)
- Pita or flatbread, for serving

Instructions:

1. Preheat the grill to medium-high heat.
2. Mix the ground lamb, onion, garlic, cumin, coriander, cinnamon, paprika, salt, and pepper in a bowl.
3. Shape the mixture into small oval or cylindrical kofta shapes.
4. Grill the kofta for 4-5 minutes per side, until browned and cooked through.
5. Serve with pita or flatbread, garnished with fresh parsley.

Grilled Flank Steak

Ingredients:

- 1 flank steak (about 1.5 lbs)
- 2 tbsp olive oil
- 1 tbsp soy sauce
- 1 tbsp balsamic vinegar
- 2 cloves garlic, minced
- 1 tsp ground cumin
- Salt and pepper to taste

Instructions:

1. Preheat the grill to medium-high heat.
2. In a bowl, mix olive oil, soy sauce, balsamic vinegar, garlic, cumin, salt, and pepper.
3. Marinate the flank steak in the mixture for at least 30 minutes.
4. Grill the steak for 4-6 minutes per side, until medium-rare (or longer for desired doneness).
5. Let the steak rest for 5 minutes before slicing against the grain.
6. Serve with a side of roasted vegetables or a fresh salad.

BBQ Baby Back Ribs

Ingredients:

- 2 racks of baby back ribs
- 1/4 cup olive oil
- 1/4 cup apple cider vinegar
- 1/4 cup brown sugar
- 1 tbsp garlic powder
- 1 tbsp onion powder
- 2 tbsp smoked paprika
- 1 tbsp ground mustard
- Salt and pepper to taste
- 1 cup BBQ sauce (for glazing)

Instructions:

1. Preheat the grill to medium-low heat.
2. Remove the membrane from the ribs and rub them with olive oil and apple cider vinegar.
3. In a bowl, combine brown sugar, garlic powder, onion powder, smoked paprika, ground mustard, salt, and pepper. Rub the spice mix evenly over the ribs.
4. Place the ribs on the grill, bone side down, and cook over indirect heat for about 2-2.5 hours, flipping occasionally.
5. In the last 15-20 minutes of cooking, brush the ribs with BBQ sauce and continue grilling until caramelized and tender.
6. Remove from the grill and rest for 5 minutes before slicing.

Grilled Duck Legs

Ingredients:

- 4 duck legs
- 2 tbsp olive oil
- 1 tbsp soy sauce
- 1 tbsp honey
- 1 tbsp fresh rosemary, chopped
- 2 cloves garlic, minced
- Salt and pepper to taste

Instructions:

1. Preheat the grill to medium heat.
2. In a bowl, whisk together olive oil, soy sauce, honey, rosemary, garlic, salt, and pepper.
3. Rub the duck legs with the marinade and let them sit for 30 minutes.
4. Grill the duck legs over indirect heat for 1-1.5 hours, turning occasionally, until the skin is crispy and the internal temperature reaches 165°F (74°C).
5. Serve with roasted vegetables or a citrus salad.

BBQ Mutton Chops

Ingredients:

- 8 mutton chops
- 2 tbsp olive oil
- 1 tbsp ground cumin
- 1 tbsp ground coriander
- 1 tsp turmeric
- 1 tsp smoked paprika
- 1/2 tsp cayenne pepper
- Salt and pepper to taste
- 1/2 cup BBQ sauce

Instructions:

1. Preheat the grill to medium-high heat.
2. In a bowl, mix olive oil, cumin, coriander, turmeric, smoked paprika, cayenne pepper, salt, and pepper.
3. Rub the mutton chops with the spice mix and let them marinate for at least 30 minutes.
4. Grill the chops for 4-6 minutes per side until they reach your preferred doneness.
5. In the last few minutes, baste the chops with BBQ sauce.
6. Serve with a side of grilled vegetables or a tangy salad.

Grilled Chicken Kebabs

Ingredients:

- 2 chicken breasts, cut into 1-inch cubes
- 1 bell pepper, cut into chunks
- 1 red onion, cut into chunks
- 2 tbsp olive oil
- 2 tbsp lemon juice
- 1 tbsp garlic powder
- 1 tbsp dried oregano
- Salt and pepper to taste
- Wooden or metal skewers

Instructions:

1. Preheat the grill to medium heat.
2. In a bowl, combine olive oil, lemon juice, garlic powder, oregano, salt, and pepper.
3. Thread the chicken, bell pepper, and onion onto the skewers, alternating between the chicken and vegetables.
4. Grill the skewers for 10-12 minutes, turning occasionally, until the chicken is fully cooked and has grill marks.
5. Serve with a side of rice or a fresh cucumber salad.

Grilled Tri-Tip Roast

Ingredients:

- 1 tri-tip roast (about 2 pounds)
- 2 tbsp olive oil
- 1 tbsp garlic powder
- 1 tbsp onion powder
- 1 tbsp smoked paprika
- 1 tsp ground cumin
- Salt and pepper to taste

Instructions:

1. Preheat the grill to medium-high heat.
2. Rub the tri-tip roast with olive oil, garlic powder, onion powder, smoked paprika, cumin, salt, and pepper.
3. Grill the tri-tip for 25-30 minutes, turning occasionally, until the internal temperature reaches 130°F (54°C) for medium-rare.
4. Let the roast rest for 10 minutes before slicing against the grain.
5. Serve with grilled vegetables or a fresh green salad.

BBQ Shredded Beef

Ingredients:

- 2 lbs beef chuck roast
- 1 onion, chopped
- 3 cloves garlic, minced
- 1 tbsp chili powder
- 1 tbsp smoked paprika
- 1 tsp cumin
- 1 tsp ground coriander
- 2 cups beef broth
- 1 cup BBQ sauce

Instructions:

1. Preheat the grill to medium-low heat.
2. Season the beef roast with chili powder, smoked paprika, cumin, coriander, salt, and pepper.
3. Sear the roast on all sides over direct heat for 4-5 minutes per side.
4. Move the roast to indirect heat and add the chopped onion and garlic. Cover the grill and cook for 2.5-3 hours, or until the beef is tender and shreds easily.
5. Shred the beef with two forks and mix in BBQ sauce.
6. Serve on sandwiches or as a main dish with sides.

Grilled Teriyaki Chicken

Ingredients:

- 4 chicken breasts
- 1/4 cup soy sauce
- 2 tbsp honey
- 1 tbsp rice vinegar
- 1 tbsp sesame oil
- 2 cloves garlic, minced
- 1 tsp grated ginger
- Sesame seeds (for garnish)

Instructions:

1. Preheat the grill to medium heat.
2. In a bowl, whisk together soy sauce, honey, rice vinegar, sesame oil, garlic, and ginger.
3. Marinate the chicken breasts in the mixture for at least 30 minutes.
4. Grill the chicken for 6-8 minutes per side, until fully cooked.
5. Garnish with sesame seeds and serve with steamed rice or a salad.

Grilled Ribeye Steak

Ingredients:

- 2 ribeye steaks (about 1-inch thick)
- 2 tbsp olive oil
- 2 cloves garlic, minced
- 1 tbsp fresh thyme
- Salt and pepper to taste

Instructions:

1. Preheat the grill to high heat.
2. Rub the steaks with olive oil, garlic, thyme, salt, and pepper.
3. Grill the steaks for 4-5 minutes per side for medium-rare, or longer for your desired doneness.
4. Let the steaks rest for 5 minutes before serving.

BBQ Pork Burnt Ends

Ingredients:

- 2 lbs pork belly, cut into cubes
- 1/4 cup brown sugar
- 1/4 cup paprika
- 2 tbsp garlic powder
- 1 tbsp onion powder
- 1 tsp cayenne pepper
- 1/2 cup BBQ sauce

Instructions:

1. Preheat the grill to medium heat.
2. In a bowl, combine brown sugar, paprika, garlic powder, onion powder, cayenne pepper, salt, and pepper.
3. Rub the pork belly cubes with the spice mixture.
4. Grill the pork for 1.5-2 hours, turning occasionally until they are crispy and caramelized.
5. In the last 15 minutes of grilling, brush with BBQ sauce and cook until the sauce sets.
6. Serve with extra BBQ sauce on the side.

Grilled Italian Sausages

Ingredients:

- 4 Italian sausages (mild or spicy)
- 1 tablespoon olive oil
- 1 bell pepper, sliced
- 1 red onion, sliced
- 2 cloves garlic, minced
- Salt and pepper to taste
- 1/4 cup fresh parsley, chopped (for garnish)

Instructions:

1. Preheat the grill to medium-high heat.
2. Drizzle the sausages with olive oil and season with salt and pepper.
3. Grill the sausages for 10-12 minutes, turning occasionally, until they are cooked through and have nice grill marks.
4. While the sausages are grilling, heat a skillet or grill pan on medium heat and sauté the bell pepper, onion, and garlic until tender.
5. Once the sausages are done, serve them with the sautéed vegetables and garnish with fresh parsley.

Grilled Beef Filet Mignon

Ingredients:

- 2 filet mignon steaks (6-8 oz each)
- 2 tablespoons olive oil
- 1 tablespoon fresh rosemary, chopped
- 2 cloves garlic, minced
- Salt and pepper to taste
- 1 tablespoon butter (for finishing)

Instructions:

1. Preheat the grill to high heat.
2. Brush the steaks with olive oil and season with salt, pepper, rosemary, and garlic.
3. Grill the steaks for 4-5 minutes per side for medium-rare, or longer if you prefer them cooked more.
4. In the last minute of grilling, place a pat of butter on top of each steak to melt.
5. Remove from the grill and let rest for 5 minutes before serving.

BBQ Chicken Sandwiches

Ingredients:

- 4 boneless skinless chicken breasts
- 1 cup BBQ sauce (your favorite)
- 4 hamburger buns
- 1/4 cup coleslaw (optional, for topping)
- Pickles (optional, for topping)

Instructions:

1. Preheat the grill to medium heat.
2. Season the chicken breasts with salt, pepper, and a bit of olive oil.
3. Grill the chicken for 6-7 minutes per side, brushing with BBQ sauce during the last few minutes of cooking.
4. Toast the hamburger buns on the grill for 1-2 minutes.
5. Once the chicken is done, assemble the sandwiches by placing the grilled chicken on the buns. Top with coleslaw and pickles if desired.

Grilled Cornish Hens

Ingredients:

- 2 Cornish hens, split in half
- 2 tablespoons olive oil
- 1 tablespoon fresh thyme, chopped
- 1 tablespoon fresh rosemary, chopped
- 1 lemon, cut into wedges
- 4 cloves garlic, minced
- Salt and pepper to taste

Instructions:

1. Preheat the grill to medium-high heat.
2. Rub the Cornish hens with olive oil, thyme, rosemary, garlic, salt, and pepper.
3. Grill the hens, skin-side down, for 10 minutes, then flip and continue grilling for another 15-20 minutes, until the internal temperature reaches 165°F (74°C).
4. Squeeze fresh lemon wedges over the hens while grilling to add flavor.
5. Remove from the grill and let rest for 5 minutes before serving.